Wabi Sabi

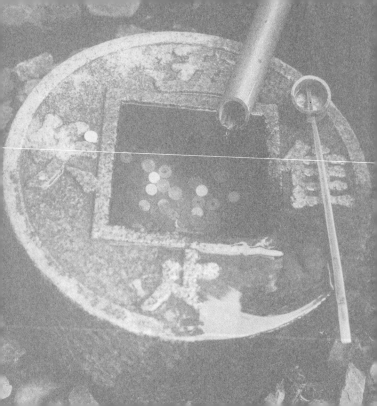

Wabi Sabi
The Art of Everyday Life

Diane Durston

Storey Publishing

The mission of Storey Publishing is to serve our customers by publishing practical information that encourages personal independence in harmony with the environment.

Edited by Nancy D. Wood and Deborah Balmuth
Art direction and cover design by Kent Lew
Text design and production by one[visual]mind
Interior photographs by John Einarsen, Karen Beck, Stephen Futscher, Paul Rocheleau, and Kent Lew (see page 360 for more credit information)
Calligraphy © Eri Takase
Text © 2006 by Diane Durston
For additional information please contact Storey Publishing, 210 MASS MoCA Way, North Adams, MA 01247. Storey books are available for special premium and promotional uses and for customized editions. For further information, please call 1-800-793-9396.

Printed in the United States by CJK
10 9 8 7 6 5 4 3 2 1

Library of Congress Cataloging-in-Publication Data
Durston, Diane, 1950–
   Wabi sabi : the art of everyday life / Diane Durston.
      p. cm.
   Includes bibliographical references and index.
   ISBN-13: 978-1-58017-628-6; ISBN-10: 1-58017-628-3 (pbk. : alk. paper)
1. Conduct of life. 2. Wabi. 3. Sabi. 4. Art and philosophy. 5. Art, Japanese. I. Title.
BJ1521.D87 2006
170'.44—dc22

                                                2006017642

For Stephen, with all my love.

The fish trap exists because of the fish.
Once you've got the fish, you can forget the trap.
The rabbit snare exists because of the rabbit.
Once you've got the rabbit, you can forget
the snare. Words exist because of meaning.
Once you've got the meaning, you can forget
the words. Where can I find a man who has
forgotten words so I can have a word with him?

— CHUANG TSE

Preface

Ink swept across the page like a brush fire — spontaneous, purposeful, and yet somehow controlled. Japanese brush painting looks simple. It is, and it is not. Years are spent achieving the ease of motion and presence of mind required in the moment the brush touches paper.

I went to Japan in 1977 to learn the skills of *sumi-e* painting, and Hidetoshi Kuwano was my first teacher. I prepared myself for this training even before I arrived in Kyoto. I read all the books. I memorized the sequence of brushstrokes required to paint a recognizable lotus (a flower I had never actually seen in nature) in the Chinese style. I had a badger-hair brush with a bamboo handle, a carved inkstone around which a mythical dragon swirled, a blue and white porcelain water dropper painted with a Chinese landscape, a stick of fragrant ink in a subtle shade of blue-black, a ream of handmade paper, and a tiny lacquered paperweight to hold it all in place. But it was not enough.

What I failed to bring was insight, the primary tool for an artist, and one that takes some time to acquire. I was to spend 18 years of my life in Japan, and none of the lessons I learned from Kuwano-sensei would be about skill. (*Sensei* means teacher or master.) He taught me instead about life and how it is lived in an Eastern culture. He taught that art is not a thing, it is a way.

By the time I left him, I had learned to at least ask the right question: "Why are you here?" This is the point of departure for an exploration of *wabi* and *sabi* — a pair of Japanese words that have come to define the best aspects of one of the world's most fascinating cultures. What I know of wabi and sabi, I learned from Kuwano-sensei and the many other amazing people I encountered in Kyoto: a shopkeeper's wife, a bamboo craftsman, a combmaker, a Zen priest, an old farmer, and a young girl sobbing in a garden.

People who know me laugh when they hear I have written a book about wabi sabi, the "essence of tranquility." My life just isn't. I can, from time to time, however, go to a place in my mind where the people I had the privilege to know in Japan keep whispering in my ear. It is my sincere hope that through the words that follow, you will hear them whispering, too.

The Concepts of Wabi and Sabi

Wabi has been defined variously in English as: tranquil simplicity; austere elegance; unpolished, imperfect, or irregular beauty; rusticity; things in their simplest, most austere, and natural state; a serene, transcendental state of mind.

Likewise, *sabi* has been interpreted as the beauty that treasures the passage of time, and with it the lonely sense of impermanence it evokes. It has also been defined as the patina that age bestows, or as that which is true to the natural cycle of birth and death.

First appearing as poetic references in Japanese literature, both wabi and sabi are closely associated with the tea ceremony, a spiritual practice invented by Zen Buddhist priests in the 15th century. Okakura

Kakuzo, who wrote the first *Book of Tea* in English one hundred years ago, defined the tea ceremony simply as "the art of everyday life."

The tea ceremony is considered a means of achieving enlightenment and peace of mind through the simple, everyday preparation of tea. The focus is on sharing a quiet moment with friends in an atmosphere of mutual respect, in an environment that reflects the quiet beauty of nature. The tea host and her guests reflect on the importance of appreciating each moment as it passes, within the greater flow of our brief and often chaotic lives. Life, therefore, becomes art; wabi and sabi are manifestations of both.

Every object in the tea ceremony plays a role. A rustic tea bowl is a reminder that nothing in life is perfect. The empty sweep of space in a scroll painting suggests that incompleteness can inspire the imagination of the beholder. A single flower in a bamboo vase invites you to take time to notice its understated beauty. The pristine finish of an unvarnished cedar box reminds you that wood will always be more beautiful than plastic. The patina that a bronze kettle acquires over time hints that we, too, will change as we pass through time.

To Sen no Rikyu, the man who brought the Way of Tea to the height of refinement in the 16th century, the ceremony is nothing more (or less) than this:

> *Make a delicious bowl of tea; lay the charcoal so it heats the water; arrange flowers as they are in the field; in summer suggest coolness, in winter, warmth; do everything ahead of time; prepare for rain; and give to those with whom you find yourself every consideration.*

"How hard can this be?" one of his students asked, to which Rikyu replied, "Well, if you can master that, you can teach me."

Wabi and sabi reflect this mindful approach to everyday life. Over time, multi-layered and heavily nuanced meanings overlapped and converged until they became almost interchangeable. Based on shared assumptions about the nature of art and life, wabi and sabi are widely accepted concepts in Japan. With both aesthetic and philosophical meanings, they are perceived as too vast to explain or define precisely.

Today's interpretation of wabi sabi as a unified concept was eloquently defined in English by Leonard Koren more than a decade ago as the "beauty of things imperfect, impermanent, and incomplete … a beauty of things modest and humble … a beauty of things unconventional." The concept made its debut in recent years in the international world of design, and a new generation of Japanese artists has begun to re-examine the underlying notions of wabi and sabi, ideas that had been pushed aside during the westernization of Japan.

The deeply human feelings about art and life that inform wabi sabi are universal, as the passages and quotes in this book from various cultures and times suggest. From teahouse to 21st-century design, the concepts of wabi and sabi continue to evolve and inspire. 🌿

wabi

The Young Girl

The painter's garden belongs in the rain.
Not a place of brilliant sunlight, it is often
sadly gray — like an older woman whose
fading beauty prompts you to remark
how beautiful she must have been. Today,
a sense of quiet melancholy clings like
crows to wet pine branches.

    In the midsummer rain, the leaves are
greener and the moss fluorescent against
wet stones hewn two centuries ago by

masons forgotten in their own time.
Kempt, but unkempt, the garden has
a mind of its own. The trees are taller
now than planned. Things die and are
replaced. Branches break and fish get
old and scarred. A heron appears like a
ghost in a dream, rests on the bridge for a
moment, and is gone.

Sit on the porch for a while and watch
the rain drizzle across the silent pond.
The master, long gone, designed it for
days like this. He understood the beauty

of the fleeting moment. Feel the rain. Let it dampen your hands and face. Watch it drip from the roofs of thatched tea huts into the muddy pond. Sit here in silence on a damp autumn afternoon, surrounded by poetry and art, frozen in this moment — enough to make a young girl cry. 🍃

Wabi is a brushwood gate,
And for a lock,
This snail.

The Woodpecker
Keeps on in the same place;
Day is closing.

Winter desolation;
In the rain water tub,
Sparrows are walking.

— ALAN WATTS

Wabi is like the feeling
of the evening sky in autumn,
somber of color,
hushed of all sound.
Somehow, as if for reasons
one should be able to call to mind,
tears begin to flow uncontrollably.

— KAMO NO CHOMEI

Wabi is the expression of beauty that is a manifestation of the creative energy that flows through all things animate and inanimate. It is a beauty that, just as nature itself, is both dark and light, sad and joyful, harsh and gentle. The beauty of this natural force is not perfect — always changing and just out of reach.

— MAKOTO UEDA

Wabi is a state of mind.

— Genjitsu (Soshitsu XV) Sen

Wabi means that which fails to satisfy, wholly refuses to submit to one's aims, and goes against what was wished. Take to heart that wabi is not considering one's incapacities, nor even embracing the thought that being ill-provided for is in any way out of the order of things.

— *The Zencharoku*

Casting wide my gaze
I see neither flowers
Nor crimson leaves:
A solitary fisherman's hut
On the twilight shore
Of this autumn eve.

— Fujiwara Teika

Instead of just grumbling about one's dire straits, detesting one's poverty, or even struggling to free oneself of this want, to conversely take such extremes of material hardship and not to be constricted by the material side, transforming it all the more into a new-found realm of spiritual freedom, to not get caught up in worldly values, but to enjoy a tranquility beyond the everyday world, this is the life of the true devotee to wabi.

— HAGA KOSHIRO

13

sabi

We do love things that bear the marks of grime, soot, and weather, and we love colors and sheen that call to mind the past that made them.

— TANIZAKI JUNICHIRO

The Basketweaver

On a stool just inside his old wooden shop front, Shintaro Morita sits slicing bamboo. His tool was made by his grandfather from the handle of a samurai sword found in a flea market 70 years ago. In telling the tale of the sword, Shintaro reveals that smashed river crabs are the best cure for hives, should you break out when working with natural lacquer. Something to remember, his grandfather had always said.

Today, Morita-san weaves magic in a flower basket from strips of *susu-dake*. The strips are made from scorched bamboo poles salvaged from the ceilings of old Japanese farmhouses, whose only source of heat was an open hearth in the middle of the room. Rising smoke tempered the bamboo, coloring it black as soot — except in places where the hemp twine bound the poles to the ceiling.

When the poles are taken down and gently burnished, an exquisite patina appears, with diagonal streaks in shades of caramel, amber, and rust. Split and shaved into bendable lengths, the *susu-dake* can then be formed into rustic containers for flowers to be displayed at a tea ceremony. No two pieces of this material are alike.

"Real *susu-dake* is hard to get these days," the craftsman complains. "There aren't many of the old farmhouses left. Some of the baskets you see now are made with ordinary bamboo that's been stained to duplicate the natural patina. Can't be done. A real tea master can always tell the difference." 🌿

Wooden temples and statues of a thousand years ago survive in Japan, having seemingly acquired permanence despite their materials, but the attempt was never consciously made to achieve the deathlessness of marble or to defy the ravages of time. Whatever has survived has aged, and the faded quality, the reminder of impermanence despite long survival, has been especially prized.

— DONALD KEENE

When the mood of the moment is
solitary and quiet, it is called sabi.
Sabi is loneliness in the sense of
Buddhist detachment, as seeing all
things as happening "by themselves"
in miraculous spontaneity.

— ALAN WATTS

Sabi … is a poetic mood vaguely pointing toward a certain view of life. This view of life is called wabi. Wabi originally meant "sadness of poverty." But gradually it came to mean an attitude toward life, with which one tried to resign himself to straitened living and to find peace and serenity of mind even under such circumstances. *Sabi*, primarily an aesthetic concept, is closely related to *wabi*, a philosophical idea.

— MAKOTO UEDA

Matsuo Basho

Down through the dark cypress forests, the call of a solitary cuckoo awakens the poet from a restless sleep. From his hut on the mountainside, the haiku master holds the entire valley in his view — and yet its essence somehow still escapes him. He lights the lamp, and fumbles for his brush:

> *Though I am in Kyoto*
> *I long for Kyoto —*
> > *Song of the night bird.*

With these words, Matsuo Basho, the wandering poet, records a indefinable sense of longing — for an ancient city perhaps, for an entire civilization, for an ideal. He grasps a beauty that is at once exquisite and unattainable. Basho captures a need we all share, for an enlightened place or a moment in time. He misses "Kyoto" — not the city, but the dream.

With ages come the inner, the higher life. Who would be forever young, to dwell always in externals?

— Elizabeth Cady Stanton

Fewer and fewer Americans possess objects that have a patina, old furniture, grandparents' pots and pans — the used things, warm with generations of human touch ... essential to a human landscape.

— SUSAN SONTAG

impermanence

To what shall I compare
this world? To the white
wake behind a ship that
has rowed away
at dawn?

— PRIEST MANSEI

The Young Monk

In the quiet frost of daybreak, a young
monk swishes the last leaves of autumn
from the stone path — into a pile of
smoldering dreams. Every last one goes
up in a spindle of smoke, twisting and
writhing through tall pines to freedom
in the morning sky.

How he envies the unfettered ascent
of leaves becoming air. He's been up since
4 A.M., his frozen pink toes pretending not

to ache in straw sandals. The chanting of the monks echoes down the empty streets of Kyoto, "Ho-o-o-o … Ho-o-o-o …" Early-rising housewives prepare their offerings to drop into the beggars' bowls.

A shaved head, dark robes, and today's lessons in selflessness — a difficult path for a restless young man who just inherited his family's country temple. He's been sent to train at Nanzenji, a famous Zen monastery at the eastern edge of the city of Kyoto.

Each day he begs for alms, polishes the wooden corridors of the temple, and rakes leaves in the courtyard — all before breakfast. He ponders this Zen riddle: Is not change the only thing that is changeless? 🌿

The world is fleeting;
all things pass away;
Or is it we that pass
and they that stay?

— LUCIAN

A ruin is not just
something that happened
long ago to someone else;
its history is that of
us all, the transience of
power, of ideas, of all
human endeavors.

— GEORGE SCHALLER

Our lives … are but a little while, so let them run as sweetly as you can, and give no thought to grief from day to day. For time is not concerned to keep our hopes, but hurries on its business, and is gone.

— EURIPEDES

By the roadside grew

A rose of Sharon.

My horse

Has just eaten it.

— Matsuo Basho

Are we to look at cherry blossoms only in full bloom, the moon only when it is cloudless? To long for the moon while looking on the rain, to lower the blinds and be unaware of the passing of spring — these are even more deeply moving. Branches about to bloom or gardens strewn with faded flowers are worthier of our admiration .... In all things, it is the beginnings and endings that are interesting.

— YOSHIDA KENKO

42

43

The Ten-Foot-Square Hut

The flow of the river is ceaseless;
and its water is never the same.
The foam that floats in the pools
Now gathering, now vanishing
Never lasts long. So it is with man
and all his dwelling places on this earth.

— KAMO NO CHOMEI

The man who wrote this poem lived in
Kyoto in a time when the chaos of war,

earthquakes, famines, floods, and fires engulfed the city. Chomei took the vows of a Buddhist priest and went off to live in a rustic mountain shack. There he spent his days writing poetry, walking in the woods, and contemplating the tragedies and simple pleasures of life. In 1212, he wrote the *Hojoki*, a moving record of the disasters of his time and of his solitary life in *The Ten-Foot-Square Hut*. The book opens with this poem, Chomei's meditation on the impermanence of life. 🌿

Have no fear
of perfection.
You'll never reach it.

— SALVADOR DALI

In a gust of wind the white dew on the Autumn grass scatters like a broken necklace.

— BUNYA NO ASAYASU

Nothing is secure but life, transition, the energizing spirit … People wish to be settled; only so far as they are unsettled is there any hope for them.

— RALPH WALDO EMERSON

Live each season as
it passes; breathe the air,
drink the drink, taste the
fruit, and resign yourself
to the influences of each.

— HENRY DAVID THOREAU

A permanent sta
transition is n
most noble cond

— JUAN RAMÓN

Nothing is secure but life, transition, the energizing spirit ... People wish to be settled; only so far as they are unsettled is there any hope for them.

— RALPH WALDO EMERSON

Live each season as
it passes; breathe the air,
drink the drink, taste the
fruit, and resign yourself
to the influences of each.

— HENRY DAVID THOREAU

A permanent state of **transition** is man's most noble condition.

— Juan Ramón Jiménez

In a gust of wind the
white dew on the
Autumn grass scatters
like a broken necklace.

— Bunya no Asayasu

The Ten-Foot-Square Hut

The flow of the river is ceaseless;
and its water is never the same.
The foam that floats in the pools
Now gathering, now vanishing
Never lasts long. So it is with man
and all his dwelling places on this earth.

— KAMO NO CHOMEI

The man who wrote this poem lived in
Kyoto in a time when the chaos of war,

earthquakes, famines, floods, and fires engulfed the city. Chomei took the vows of a Buddhist priest and went off to live in a rustic mountain shack. There he spent his days writing poetry, walking in the woods, and contemplating the tragedies and simple pleasures of life. In 1212, he wrote the *Hojoki*, a moving record of the disasters of his time and of his solitary life in *The Ten-Foot-Square Hut*. The book opens with this poem, Chomei's meditation on the impermanence of life. ❧

Have no fear
of perfection.
You'll never reach it.

— SALVADOR DALI

To be interested in the changing seasons is a happier state of mind than to be hopelessly in love with spring.

— George Santayana

Transience and limits are at the core of our nature, and you can consider that a curse or a blessing. Our lives are less than atomic flickers on the scale of the cosmos, but they would be equally infinitesimal if they lasted 10 million times longer, and they would still be infinitely precious to us. You have the chance to enjoy some morsel of the 10^{14} years that the sun and stars will last. You should.

— JOHN RENNIE

In the presence
of eternity, the
mountains are as
transient as the clouds.

— ROBERT GREEN INGERSOLL

The Fleeting World

If man were never to fade away but lingered
on forever in the world, how things would
lose their power to move us! The most precious
thing in life is its uncertainty. Consider living
creatures — none lives so long as man. The
May fly waits not for evening, the summer
cicada knows neither spring nor autumn.
What a wonderfully unhurried feeling it is
to live even a single year in perfect serenity!
If that is not enough for you, you might live a

thousand years and still feel it is but a single night's dream.

Legend has it that *Tsurezuregusa* (*Essays in Idleness*) was written on scraps of paper that the author, Yoshida Kenko, pasted to the walls of his cottage. Years later, a thoughtful friend carefully removed the scraps, thus collecting one of the greatest works of Japanese literature. The 243 episodes of this 14th-century classic capture the essence of the fleeting nature of the world. 🌿

What is life? It is the flash of a firefly in the night. It is the breath of a buffalo in the wintertime. It is the little shadow which runs across the grass and loses itself in the sunset.

— CROWFOOT

Life is a candle

before the wind.

— JAPANESE PROVERB

Would that life were like
the shadow cast by a wall
or a tree, but it is like the
shadow of a bird
in flight.

— *Haggadah*, PALESTINIAN TALMUD

In three words I can
sum up everything I've
learned about life:
it goes on.

— ROBERT FROST

Life is but a day;
A fragile dew-drop
on its perilous way
From a tree's summit.

— JOHN KEATS

Security is mostly a superstition. It does not exist in nature, nor do the children of men as a whole experience it. Avoiding danger is no safer in the long run than outright exposure. Life is either a daring adventure or nothing.

— HELEN KELLER

Mujo (Impermanence)

There is an hour or so in the fall
when the sky is clear and sharp
when the clouds move predictably
refusing to gather into storms
when a crisp confidence
in the fullness of its own beauty
resounds in the Mountain's colors

as if, in this moment,
the trees do not fear
the inevitable approach of Winter.
They know all about that
fly-by-night Imposter masquerading
with the face of Death. 🍂

imperfection

The Master Craftsman

Kuroda Kenkichi was a master of the art of fine woodworking. The eldest son of a renowned craftsman, he spent most of his life in his father's shadow. Born in 1935, he would play in the sawdust on the floor of his father's workshop, where great artist-philosophers of the day gathered. There they would sit, in endless dialogue on the materialism they believed was destroying the spirit of Japan.

IMPERFECTION

It was not Kenkichi's ambition, however, to achieve the perfect polished wood surface for which his father was so famous. Years of a struggling apprenticeship would be involved, and he wanted none of it. His plan was to get a motorcycle and cruise the streets, free from the restraints his father's trade would place on his freedom.

Somewhere amid the motorcycles and a carefree life gone wrong, the young man lost himself and returned to his father's house. He went on to become a remarkable craftsman, but he was not to carry on the family name. Though it went against tradition, his father gave that honor to his younger brother, who lacked a certain passion for life, but had remained faithful to the family trade.

"I found out there is freedom within restraint," he would later tell the motley young apprentices who gathered around the table in his modest tatami-mat parlor. The lessons life had taught him touched souls — foreign and Japanese — that his illustrious father never reached. Before Kenkichi died, he had trained a superb apprentice who now carries on the craft at the highest level of achievement and recognition.

In the center of his table, there always sat an unassuming lacquered container, the first wooden object he had finished on his own. The pot was carved from a solid piece of *keyaki*, hexagonal in shape. The wiped-lacquer finish had incomparable depth and beauty. But the lid

was slightly warped — it wasn't perfect.
"Oh? Do you really like it?" he asked,
though the grain and luster of that wood
has not left my memory in all the years
that have passed. 🌿

The most valued bowls for tea
ceremony are irregularly shaped, and
some have gold patches here and there
accentuating (rather than concealing)
damage suffered at the hands of
long-ago owners. Asymmetry and
irregularity allow the possibility
of growth, but perfection
chokes the imagination.

— DONALD KEENE

In everything, no matter what it may be, uniformity is undesirable. Leaving something incomplete makes it interesting and gives one the feeling that there is room for growth.

— *Tsurezuregusa*,
YOSHIDA KENKO

The artist who aims at
perfection in everything
achieves it in nothing.

— Eugène Delacroix

Perfection has one
grave defect:
it is apt to be dull.

— WILLIAM SOMERSET MAUGHAM

The principle mark of genius is not perfection but originality, the opening of new frontiers.

— ARTHUR KOESTLER

Ring the bells that still can ring

Forget your perfect offering

There is a crack in everything

That's how the light gets in.

— LEONARD COHEN

Striving for **excellence** motivates you; striving for perfection is demoralizing.

— HARRIET BERYL BRAIKER

In Praise of Shadows

Born in 1886, decades after Japan opened its ports to the West, Tanizaki Junichiro was obsessed with his country's traditional past. He rejected what he saw as the superficial westernization that was taking place all around him. The work for which he is best known in the West is a short essay titled *In Praise of Shadows* (1933). In it, he writes eloquently of the shadowy beauty of a traditional Japanese home:

I would call back this world of shadows we are losing. I would have the eaves deep and the walls dark, I would push back into the shadows the things that come forth too clearly, I would strip away the useless decoration. I do not ask that this be done everywhere, but perhaps we may be allowed at least one mansion where we can turn off the electric lights and see what it is like without them. 🌿

My imperfections and failures are as much a blessing from God as my successes and my talents and I lay them both at his feet.

— MAHATMA GANDHI

Better a diamond
with a flaw than a
pebble without.

— CONFUCIUS

People throw away what
they could have by
insisting on perfection,
which they cannot have,
and looking for it where
they will never find it.

— EDITH SCHAEFFER

Once you accept the fact
that you're not perfect,
then you develop some
confidence.

— ROSALYNN CARTER

Certain flaws are
necessary for the whole.
It would seem strange
if old friends lacked
certain quirks.

— GOETHE

You see, when weaving a blanket, an Indian woman leaves a flaw in the weaving of that blanket to let the soul out.

— MARTHA GRAHAM

Perfectionism

is slow death.

— HUGH PRATHER

As machines become more and more efficient and perfect, so it will become clear that imperfection is the greatness of man.

— ERNST FISCHER

Gold cannot be pure,
and people
cannot be perfect.

— CHINESE PROVERB

One of the most essential things you need to do for yourself is to choose a goal that is important to you. Perfection does not exist — you can always do better and you can always grow.

— LES BROWN

simplicity

The Shopkeeper's Wife

It is cold morning in January. Sliding open
the wood-slatted door, the first thing in
the dark interior to catch the eye is a tiny
vase. A single, perfect camellia bud hints
of light at the end of winter's tunnel —
an elegant nod to the changing season,
lest we forget in our hurry.

In the entry hall, shoes are left behind
on a concrete floor. An invitation comes to
step into a small tatami-mat room where

the Hasegawa family greets their guests. Mrs. Hasegawa appears, smiling her welcome and bowing profusely, a symbol of respect. You are an honored guest, as is everyone who crosses her threshold.

There is nothing in the room except worn paper doors and a battle-scarred wooden corner post polished smooth by the hands of four generations of hardworking merchants. Mrs. Hasegawa gestures graciously to be seated on the floor cushions she has prepared for the occasion.

"A cup of tea?" she offers. No one who knows her would refuse.

Mrs. Hasegawa is famous for what she refers to as her only vice. She manages to save a bit extra each month to support her habit of drinking the finest green tea in the world. It is a simple pleasure, and she always finds the time to share a cup of her sweetly fragrant gyokuro tea — and the warmth of her hospitality — with a special friend. 🌿

Meanwhile, let us have a sip of tea.
The afternoon is brightening the bamboo,
the fountains are bubbling with delight,
the soughing of the pines is heard in our
kettle. Let us dream of evanescence,
and linger in the beautiful
foolishness of things.

— OKAKURA TENSHIN

The aspects of things that are most important for us are hidden because of their simplicity and familiarity.

— LUDWIG WITTGENSTEIN

Simplicity is the

ultimate sophistication.

— LEONARDO DA VINCI

The ordinary acts
we practice every day
at home are of more
importance to the soul
than their simplicity
might suggest.

— THOMAS MORE

It is through creating,

not possessing, that

life is revealed.

— VIDA D. SCUDDER

The best things in life are nearest:
Breath in your nostrils, light in your
eyes, flowers at your feet, duties at your
hand, the path of right just before you.
Then do not grasp at the stars, but do life's
plain, common work as it comes, certain
that daily duties and daily bread are the
sweetest things in life.

— ROBERT LOUIS STEVENSON

A man is rich in proportion to the number of things which he can afford to let alone.

— HENRY DAVID THOREAU

A Cottage Beside a Pond

In spring 1845, Henry David Thoreau
built a wooden hut on the shores of
Walden Pond in Concord, Massachusetts.
He was familiar with the writings of
Eastern philosophers, and with Ralph
Waldo Emerson. A leader of the Transcen-
dentalist movement, his writings had a
powerful impact on the way Americans
feel about nature and the environment
— and about the choices each person

must make about how to spend this time
on earth.

I say, let your affairs be as two or three, and not
a hundred or a thousand; instead of a million,
count half a dozen, and keep your accounts
on your thumbnail. In the midst of this chop-
ping sea of civilized life, such are the clouds and
storms and quicksands and thousand-and-one
items to be allowed for, that a man has to live,
if he would not founder and go to the bottom
and not make his port at all, by dead reckoning,

and he must be a great calculator indeed who
succeeds. Simplify, simplify. Instead of three
meals a day, if it be necessary eat but one;
instead of a hundred dishes, five; and reduce
other things in proportion. ❧

Have nothing
in your house
that you do not
know to be useful,
or believe to be
beautiful.

— WILLIAM MORRIS

Be content with what
you have, rejoice in
the way things are.
When you realize there
is nothing lacking,
the whole world
belongs to you.

— LAO TSE

If one's life is simple, contentment has to come. Simplicity is extremely important for happiness. Having few desires, feeling satisfied with what you have, is very vital: satisfaction with just enough food, clothing, and shelter to protect yourself from the elements. And finally, there is an intense delight in abandoning faulty states of mind and in cultivating helpful ones in meditation.

— HIS HOLINESS THE DALAI LAMA

I believe that a simple and unassuming manner of life is best for everyone, best both for the body and the mind.

— ALBERT EINSTEIN

Whatever we treasure
for ourselves separates us
from others; our possessions
are our limitations.

— RABINDRANATH TAGORE

Adopt the pace of nature;
her secret is patience.
Sometimes you don't need
the things you "need"
to enjoy the simple
things, quiet times,
friends, family.

— AMISH PROVERB

Life is really simple,
but men insist on
making it complicated.

— CONFUCIUS

A certain degree of physical
harmony and comfort is necessary,
but above a certain level it becomes a
hindrance instead of a help. Therefore
the ideal of creating an unlimited
number of wants and satisfying them
seems to be a delusion and a snare.

— MAHATMA GANDHI

All of Nature
in a Single Blossom

One of the best-loved stories about Sen no
Rikyu, the revered 16th-century tea master,
involves his relationship with Hideyoshi
Toyotomi, a great warlord, whom he served
as an advisor on matters of art and taste.
Upon hearing of an exquisite display of
morning glories in Rikyu's garden, the warlord asked to see it. To honor the request,
one morning Rikyu invited him to tea.

As the warlord walked down the garden path, there were no flowers anywhere to be seen. When he entered the tea hut, however, his eyes were drawn to a single morning glory displayed in the alcove. Rikyu had ordered all the morning glories in the garden to be cut down that morning to focus his lordship's attention on the single exquisite blossom. 🌿

How simple and frugal a thing is happiness: a glass of wine, a roast chestnut, a wretched little brazier, the sound of the sea …. All that is required to feel that here and now is happiness is a simple, frugal heart.

— NIKOS KAZANTZAKIS

Wealth consists not in having great possessions, but in having few wants.

— EPICTETUS

Any intelligent fool can make things bigger, more complex, and more violent. It takes a touch of genius — and a lot of courage — to move in the opposite direction.

— E. F. Schumacher

To find the universal elements enough; to find the air and the water exhilarating; to be refreshed by a morning walk or an evening saunter; to be thrilled by the stars at night; to be elated over a bird's nest or a wildflower in spring — these are some of the rewards of the simple life.

— JOHN BURROUGHS

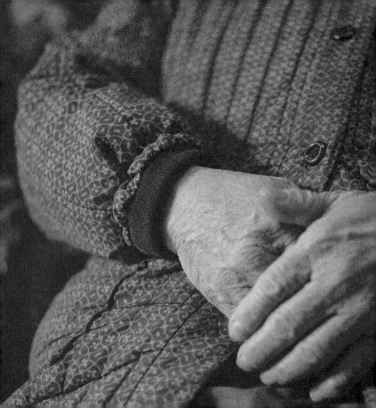

humility

The Bucket Maker

Splitting another cedar stave by hand, Mr. Tomii grins patiently at his guests as he demonstrates the process of making Japanese bath buckets — the kind almost no one uses anymore. Seated on the floor of his cramped old shop front, he uses both fingers and toes to make wooden buckets in the old way. Planed by hand with his grandfather's tools and painstakingly joined with bamboo pegs, each cedar stave is shaved smooth and left unvarnished — a clean, natural beauty wrought by the unselfconscious hands of one of the last of the real artisans.

The elderly in this old neighborhood are the only ones who use his buckets the way they were intended. A few are still frugal enough to bring him their worn-out wash buckets to be repaired, and he loves them for it. Some of them refuse to use washing machines — it just doesn't seem to get the dirt out properly. Washing kimono silk

the old way in a wooden tub keeps
the older women moving, keeps their
traditions alive.

   Today, Tomii-san leads his curious
foreign visitors out to the back of the
creaking 100-year-old, tile-roofed house,
past the bottomless old well, the rustic
wood-burning stove and the impromptu
outdoor shower. He will never see the
things they can't live without: the dish-
washers, garbage disposals, and walk-in
closets. He has no interest in them. He

tells them that he is interested only in making wooden buckets until he dies.

With no heir and no apprentice, he sips his sakè and waits alone each night for dawn to give him another day with his precious wood, another day to smile and teach us what it means to love our work. 🌿

Humility,
that low, sweet root,
From which all heavenly
virtues shoot.

— THOMAS MOORE

There is something
in humility which
strangely exalts the heart.

— SAINT AUGUSTINE

I have three precious things
which I hold fast and prize.
The first is gentleness; the second
is frugality; the third is humility,
which keeps me from putting myself
before others. Be gentle and you can be
bold; be frugal and you can be liberal;
avoid putting yourself before others and
you can become a leader among men.

— LAO TSE

I really love my
barrel-making job;
connecting each board
into one round barrel.

— ZEN FOLK SAYING

It is not the man who
has too little, but the
man who craves more,
who is poor.

— Lucius Annaeus Seneca

It is far more impressive when others discover your good qualities without your help.

— Judith Martin

Pride makes us
artificial and
humility makes
us real.

— THOMAS MERTON

I claim to be a simple individual liable to err like any other fellow mortal. I own, however, that I have humility enough to confess my errors and to retrace my steps.

— MAHATMA GANDHI

Frugality is one of the most beautiful and joyful words in the English language, and yet one that we are culturally cut off from understanding and enjoying. The consumption society has made us feel that happiness lies in having things, and has failed to teach us the happiness of not having things.

— Elise Boulding

When science discovers the center of the universe, a lot of people will be disappointed to find they are not it.

— BERNARD BAILEY

The Spirit of
the Unknown Craftsman

After 250 years of self-imposed isolation, Japan was opened to the West in 1852 by foreign powers seeking world trade. From then on, the introverted country embraced, one by one, the remarkable accomplishments of Western civilization. Everything "old" was rejected as outdated and primitive.

In the 1920s, a small group of artists and craftsmen, led by scholar Yanagi Soetsu, came together to remind their fellow countrymen of the value of things that were being lost. They believed that objects produced by anonymous craftsmen have a "pure innocence" that speaks of a universal human spirit. Common clay rice bowls, rough-cut bamboo vases, and hand-woven fish baskets are a gentle reminder of a common humanity. This can put them in touch — for just a moment in a busy day — with that greater meaning of life we all share. Humility is not cowardice. It is the recognition that we are all equal and all worthy of respect, whether we be rich or poor, great or small.

Humility makes great
men twice honorable.

— Benjamin Franklin

What I see in Nature is a magnificent structure that we can comprehend only very imperfectly, and that must fill a thinking person with a feeling of humility. This is a genuinely religious feeling that has nothing to do with mysticism.

— ALBERT EINSTEIN

When pride comes,
then comes disgrace,
but with humility
comes wisdom.

— PROVERBS 11:2

Personally, I rather look forward to

a computer program winning

the world chess championship.

Humanity needs a lesson in humility.

— RICHARD DAWKINS

It is a wholesome and necessary thing
for us to turn again to the earth and in the
contemplation of her beauties to know of
wonder and humility.

— RACHEL CARSON

True humility is contentment. There is no respect for others without humility in one's self.

— HENRI FRÉDÉRIC AMIEL

Answering
Your Own Questions

What America knows of the ideas and philosophy of Zen Buddhism is due in large part to the life and work of Daisetsu Teitaro Suzuki. In 1938, he wrote that the Zen master does not believe that the meaning of life can be understood intellectually; he believes in realizing peace through the everyday experiences of life. Suzuki told the following Zen story of Tenno Dogo.

Dogo had a disciple called Soshin. When Soshin was taken in as a novice, it was perhaps natural of him to expect lessons in Zen from his teacher the way a school boy is taught at school. But Dogo gave him no special lessons on the subject, and this bewildered and disappointed Soshin. One day he said to the master, "It is some time since I came here, but not a word has been given me regarding the essence of the Zen teaching." Dogo replied, "Since your arrival I have ever been giving you lessons on the matter of Zen discipline."

"What kind of lesson could it have been?"

"When you bring me a cup of tea in the morning, I take it; when you serve me a meal, I accept it; when you bow to me, I return it with a nod. How else do you expect to be taught in the mental discipline of Zen?"

Soshin hung his head for a while, pondering the puzzling words of the master. The master said, "If you want to see, see right at once. When you begin to think, you miss the point."

A man wrapped up
in himself makes
a very small bundle.

— BENJAMIN FRANKLIN

It wasn't until quite late
in life that I discovered
how easy it is to say
"I don't know!"

— WILLIAM SOMERSET MAUGHAM

Earth provides enough to satisfy every man's need, but not every man's greed.

— MAHATMA GANDHI

It is preoccupation with possessions,

more than anything else, that prevents

men from living freely and nobly.

— BERTRAND RUSSELL

The best things in life aren't things.

— ART BUCHWALD

Even the most expensive

clock still shows sixty

minutes in *every* hour.

— Jewish proverb

We must rapidly begin the shift from a "thing-oriented" society to a "person-oriented" society. When machines and computers, profit motives, and property rights are considered more important than people, the giant triplets of racism, materialism, and militarism are incapable of being conquered.

— MARTIN LUTHER KING, JR.

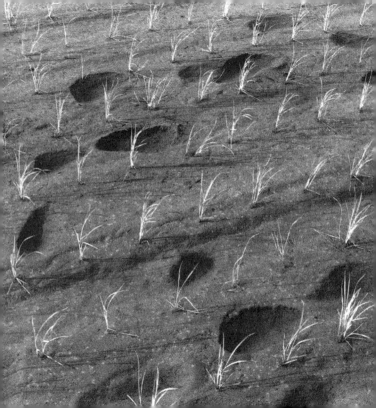

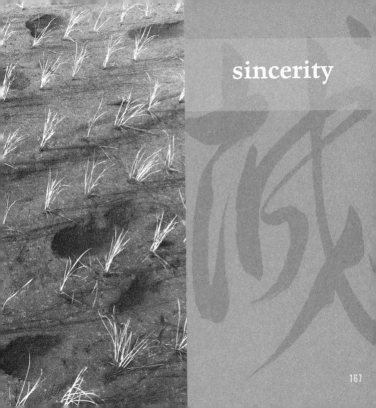

sincerity

The Painter

"Now let me see your sketchbook …
hmmm. *Inchiki!* This is cheating! You're
trying to show me how skilled you are.
Don't think about how to paint, think
about why. Your drawings should be
tiny monuments to the excellence of
humanity!"

It's a lot to learn on a Saturday afternoon. But the painting teacher drones
on and on in a language you barely

understand. If you fail to concentrate for even a moment, or let your mind stay behind for two seconds to unravel a difficult sentence, you are lost completely.

He changes the subject now to speak of kireigoto, "pretty things," meaningless things. People spend all their time acquiring things. It's an endless cycle — always wanting more and bigger. You throw away the smaller one for the larger, toss out the old one for a new one that suits your mood today.

The only lasting things are those you keep inside. This is a dark time on earth, and it's filled with bad people. No one has room in their hearts anymore for art or nature. They can't see beyond their money and their "pretty things" — they've forgotten how to enjoy their short lives, forgotten how to dream. This makes it all the more important for you to become just the opposite. You must be sincere. 🌿

To send light into the
darkness of men's hearts
— such is the duty of
the artist.

— ROBERT A. SCHUMANN

Take back the beauty and wit you
bestow upon me; leave me my own
mediocrity of agreeableness and genius,
but leave me also my sincerity,
my constancy, and my plain dealing;
'tis all I have to recommend me to the
esteem either of others or myself.

— LADY MARY WORLEY MONTAGU

Sincerity is an openness of heart;
we find it in very few people; what we
usually see is only an artful dissimulation
to win the confidence of others.

— FRANÇOIS DE LA ROCHEFOUCAULD

Hateful to me as the
gates of Hades is that
man who hides one
thing in his heart and
speaks another.

— HOMER

"Sincerity?
I can fake that."

— HAWKEYE PIERCE

The great enemy of clear language is insincerity. When there is a gap between one's real and one's declared aims, one turns, as it were, instinctively to long words and exhausted idioms, like a cuttlefish squirting out ink.

— GEORGE ORWELL

What uttered from
the heart alone
Will win the hearts of
others to our own.

— GOETHE

Sincerity and truth

are the basis of every virtue.

— Confucius

An insincere and evil friend is

more to be feared than a wild beast;

a wild beast may wound your body,

but an evil friend will wound

your mind.

— THE BUDDHA

True humanness consists of a continuous series of tiny acts executed with absolute sincerity and largeness of heart.

— SRI SATHYA SAI BABA

Sincerity makes the
very least person
to be of more value
than the most
talented hypocrite.

— CHARLES HADDON SPURGEON

The Way of Tea

The room is ten square feet of woven tatami mats. Everything has been carefully handmade of natural materials — clay, straw, and sand; bamboo, wood, and iron. Nothing inside distracts from its function as a quiet space to spend a meditative moment. Removed for an hour or two from the chaos of everyday life, one can focus completely on this shared moment as if it were once in a lifetime: *Ichigo, ichie.*

The spareness of the room directs attention to each object within it. A single flower tossed in a rustic bamboo vase curves gracefully as if it were still in the forest. A sturdy clay tea bowl with a rough texture and mottled colors feels comfortingly imperfect in one's hands. There is the sound of water simmering in a rustic tea kettle, the fragrance of hot charcoal. The air is not "conditioned" — just warm enough not to shiver, and cool enough to relax. No more, no less.

Having prepared tea a thousand times in the same careful manner, the host flows through the motions unselfconsciously and with considerable grace. He is the essence of calm hospitality, focused solely on his guests' comfort and enjoyment. The guests are attentive, waiting for just the right moment to remark that the scroll hanging in the alcove sets just the right tone for the day. "Sincerity" it reads, nothing more. 🌿

SINCERITY

The artist must summon all his energy, his sincerity, and the greatest modesty in order to shatter the old clichés that come so easily to hand while working, which can suffocate the little flower that does not come, ever, the way one expects.

— HENRI MATISSE

It is best to be yourself,
imperial, plain and true.

— ROBERT BROWNING

No man can produce
great things who is not
thoroughly sincere
in dealing with himself.

— JAMES RUSSELL LOWELL

I sat at a table where were rich food

and wine in abundance, and obsequious

attendance, but sincerity and truth

were not; and I went away hungry

from the inhospitable board.

— HENRY DAVID THOREAU

You can play

a shoestring

if you're sincere.

— JOHN COLTRANE

The way I see it, it doesn't matter what you believe just so you're sincere.

— CHARLES M. SCHULZ

Wheresoever you go,
go with all your heart.

— CONFUCIUS

The merit of originality is not novelty;
it is sincerity. The believing man is the
original man; whatsoever he believes,
he believes it for himself, not for another.

— THOMAS CARLYLE

Sincerity is like traveling on
a plain, beaten road,
which commonly brings a man
sooner to his journey's end
than by-ways, in which men
often lose themselves.

— JOHN TILLOTSON

Be sincere,

be brief;

be seated.

— FRANKLIN D. ROOSEVELT

You know I say just what
I think, and nothing more
and less. I cannot say one
thing and mean another.

— HENRY WADSWORTH LONGFELLOW

Nothing gives rest
but the sincere search for truth.

— BLAISE PASCAL

Sincerity is the
highest complement
you can pay.

— RALPH WALDO EMERSON

harmony

The Painting Lesson

It is bitterly cold, and dreams of summer are broken by the hissing of the tea kettle on the kerosene stove. It is Saturday, the Day of the Lesson. After waiting for half an hour in the snow for the frigid, half-empty bus, you are at least happy to warm your hands by the stove and sip hot green tea while you wait for Sensei to arrive.

No sooner does the teacher enter the room and unwrap his muffler than he begins to relate what is on his mind this morning: mountain climbing. He's read in the paper about two young hikers who were rescued on the side of a frozen mountain.

It is midwinter after all, he says. They buy their fancy gear and think they are ready for the mountains. Climbing is about the strength in your hands, your balance, and the sureness of your feet. These cannot be purchased at a department store. You must know the elements you face and build endurance for this kind of cold. Well, they are down safely now. But, there is a lesson in everything. Down is the necessary opposite of up.

Let's go outside, he says. Before the Pacific War, we were very poor, you know, and we used to climb the hills to forage for food in the winter. Now take a look just beneath the snow over there. See the tips of bright green shoots peeking through? Did you know you can eat those? Tastes good, if you prepare them right.

When we first saw these shoots breaking through the snow, it reminded us that spring would come again — just when we'd nearly lost hope. You can't lose hope in hard times.

Draw that, he says. And the lesson begins.

Look deep
into nature, and
then you will
understand
everything better.

— ALBERT EINSTEIN

There is … beauty in the migration of the birds, the ebb and flow of the tides, the folded bud ready for the spring. There is something **infinitely healing** in the repeated refrains of nature — the assurance that dawn comes after night, and spring after the winter.

— RACHEL CARSON

Nature does not hurry, yet everything is accomplished.

— LAO TSE

The world is
mud-luscious and
puddle-wonderful.

— E. E. CUMMINGS

Climb up on some hill at sunrise. Everybody needs perspective once in a while, and you'll find it there.

— ROBB SAGENDORPH

You can't be suspicious of a tree, or accuse a bird or a squirrel of subversion or challenge the ideology of a violet.

— RON LARSON

The clearest way into

the universe is through

a forest wilderness.

— JOHN MUIR

Every generation
thinks it has the answers,
and every generation is
humbled by nature.

— PHILIP LUBIN

The best remedy for those who are
afraid, lonely or unhappy is to go outside,
somewhere where they can be quiet,
alone with the heavens, nature and God.
Because only then does one feel that all
is as it should be and that God wishes
to see people happy, amidst the
simple beauty of nature.

— ANNE FRANK

The richness I achieve
comes from Nature,
the source of my
inspiration.

— CLAUDE MONET

One touch of
nature makes the
whole world kin.

— WILLIAM SHAKESPEARE

I've made an odd discovery.

Every time I talk to a savant

I feel quite sure that happiness

is no longer a possibility.

Yet when I talk with my gardener,

I'm convinced of the opposite.

— BERTRAND RUSSELL

Adopt the pace of nature:

her secret is patience.

— RALPH WALDO EMERSON

There is a pleasure in the pathless woods,

There is a rapture on the lonely shore,

There is society, where none intrudes,

By the deep sea, and music in its roar:

I love not man the less, but Nature more.

— LORD BYRON

Earth's crammed
with heaven,
And every common
bush afire with God

— ELIZABETH BARRETT BROWNING

It is not so much for its beauty
that the forest makes a claim upon
men's hearts, as for that subtle something,
that quality of air, that emanation
from old trees, that so wonderfully
changes and renews a weary spirit.

— ROBERT LOUIS STEVENSON

Nature is beneficent. I praise her and all her works. She is silent and wise. She is cunning, but for good ends. She has brought me here and will also lead me away. She may scold me, but she will not hate her work. I trust her.

— GOETHE

Knowing trees,

I understand the meaning of patience.

Knowing grass,

I can appreciate persistence.

— HAL BORLAND

Wa-Kei-Sei-Jaku

The four guiding principles of the discipline of tea ceremony are: to seek *harmony* (*wa*) with nature and other human beings; to show *respect* (*kei*) for all things and people; to revere the *purity* (*sei*) of a clean and orderly environment; and to enter a state of *tranquility* (*jaku*) amid the chaotic world in which we live.

In the environment of the wabi-style tearoom, the unadorned beauty of natural materials is manifest in every utensil and furnishing. The atmosphere is calm and orderly. Guests show respect for their host and for the objects used to prepare and serve the tea. Careful attention is paid to the craftsmanship apparent in these objects. Appreciation is shown for the poetic message inscribed on the hanging scroll, which sets the theme and refers to the season.

The host in turn pays meticulous attention to the needs of his guests. Nothing extraneous is present in the room nor in the conversation which takes place. No unkind words are spoken. The tragedies and turmoil of the outside world are left outside the garden gate. For now, both host and guest reflect upon this special moment they have been given together: *ichigo, ichie* (each moment, only once).

I believe in God,

only I spell it Nature.

— FRANK LLOYD WRIGHT

If you truly love Nature,
you will find beauty
everywhere.

— Vincent van Gogh

I don't believe people are looking for the meaning of life as much as they are looking for the experience of being alive.

— JOSEPH CAMPBELL

I would rather wake
up in the middle of
nowhere than in any
city on earth.

— STEVE MCQUEEN

My father considered a walk

among the mountains

as the equivalent of churchgoing.

— ALDOUS HUXLEY

The life of man in
every part has need
of harmony
and rhythm.

— PLATO

If the sight of the blue skies

fills you with joy, if a blade of grass

springing up in the fields has power

to move you, if the simple things

in nature have a message you understand,

rejoice, for your soul is alive.

— ELEANORA DUSE

There is a way that nature speaks, that land speaks. Most of the time we are simply not patient enough, quiet enough, to pay attention to the story.

— LINDA HOGAN

The poetry of the earth

is never dead.

— JOHN KEATS

Look at the trees, look at the birds,
look at the clouds, look at the stars . . .
and if you have eyes you will be able
to see that the whole of existence is
joyful. Everything is simply happy. Trees
are happy for no reason; they are
not going to become prime ministers
or presidents and they are not going to
become rich and they will never have
any bank balance. Look at the flowers —
for no reason. It is simply unbelievable
how happy flowers are.

— Osho

Speak to the earth,
and it shall teach thee.

— JOB 12:8

purity

Purity of mind
and idleness are
incompatible.

— MAHATMA GANDHI

The Combmaker

Beneath the giant camphor trees lining
the path to the Grand Shrine of Ise walks
the unprepossessing figure of Kyoto's finest boxwood combmaker, Takeuchi Michi-
kazu. He has come to inspect the hand-cut
boxwood wedges that have been aging in
the shrine vaults for more than 10 years.
Takeuchi is preparing for the daunting
task of making a set of 91 hand-polished
boxwood combs, as offerings to the shrine.

They will replace the combs made by his father in a ritual of renewal that has been practiced for the past 1,200 years.

Today, Takeuchi-san also comes to pay his respects to the gods of this sacred forest. He asks them to give him time to finish his precious combs. He is not well; he needs another year. He picks up the bamboo ladle on the stone basin, dips it into the pure, clear water, and rinses his hands and mouth to purify his soul.

The journey to the Grand Shrine of Ise

— center of worship for the indigenous Shinto religion — is a long one, but worth it. The Sun Goddess is said to live here, as she has for 15 centuries, surrounded by virgin forest and separated from the world by the waters of Isuzu River. She lives a secluded life. Only high priests and the emperor himself may come to call.

The pristine cypress structure is assembled by hand from crisply cut, unpainted beams. The roof is topped by horned finials pointing resolutely to the sky — the only part of the shrine visible from behind the sacred enclosure. The Sacred Mirror and over 2,500 ceremonial objects are housed here, including an elegant set of combs once required to groom the elaborate hairstyles of aristocratic ladies.

Every 20 years, a unique rite of renewal takes place. Until the late 19th century, this involved the destruction and rebuilding of the shrine and all of the ceremonial objects. Today the objects are not destroyed, but kept in a special museum.

It is the greatest honor of a craftsman's life to be among those chosen to restore the shrine.

Before his illness took him, Takeuchi-san completed all 91 of the exquisite combs. They will serve the Sun Goddess for another 20 years, when Takeuchi's son will be there to replace them. ✿

A person might be an expert

in any field of knowledge or

a master of many material skills

and accomplishments. But without

inner cleanliness

his brain is a desert waste.

— Sri Sathya Sai Baba

My strength has the strength of ten, because my heart is pure.

— LORD ALFRED TENNYSON

Todo saldra en al colada.

[All will come out

in the washing.]

— Miguel de Cervantes Saavedra

As to the pure mind
all things are pure, so
to the poetic mind all
things are poetical.

— HENRY WADSWORTH LONGFELLOW

Purity is not imposed upon us as though it were a kind of punishment, it is one of those mysterious but obvious conditions of that supernatural knowledge of ourselves in the Divine, which we speak of as faith. Impurity does not destroy this knowledge, it slays our need for it.

— GEORGES BERNANOS

Notes from The Tea Master

The Japanese Way of Tea, (or *chado*), perfected in the 16th century by Sen no Rikyu, has a long and distinguished history. The honorable position of Grand Master of the Urasenke School of Tea has been passed down from Sen no Rikyu through 16 generations. Dr. Genjitsu (Soshitsu XV) Sen, the former Grand Master, wrote extensively about the Way of Tea as a vehicle for peace, extending that message to 50 countries around the world. On the importance of purity, Dr. Sen wrote:

Purity, through the simple act of cleaning, is an important part of a tea gathering — in preparation beforehand, the actual service of tea, and after the guests have left, the storing away of the utensils and the final closing of the tea-room. Such actions as clearing the dust from the room and the dead leaves from the garden path all represent clearing the "dust of the world," or the worldly attachments, from one's heart and mind. It is then, after putting aside material concerns, that people and things can be perceived in their truest state. The act of cleaning thus enables one to sense the pure and sacred essence of things, man, and nature.

When the host is cleaning and arranging the areas that the guests will occupy, he is establishing order also within himself; this order is essential. As he attends to the details of the tearoom and garden path, he is no less attending to his own consciousness and to the state of mind in which he will serve the guest. 🌿

Only the pure in heart
can make a good soup.

— LUDWIG VAN BEETHOVEN

A life of peace,
purity, and refinement
leads to a **calm** and
untroubled old age.

— Cicero

There is a strange glow on the face of a guileless person. Inner cleanliness has its own soap and water — the soap of strong faith and the water of constant practice.

— SRI SATHYA SAI BABA

Cleanliness may be
defined to be the
emblem of purity
of mind.

— JOSEPH ADDISON

The Shaker Path

The Japanese preference for simple clean lines and natural materials would have been well understood by the Shakers of New England of the 19th century. The Shakers followed a strict spiritual discipline that echoes many of the practices of Zen — the principles of frugality, cleanliness, purity, honesty, and simplicity are intrinsic to both traditions. The pure, practical beauty of a bentwood Shaker box would not be out of place in the wabi tearooms of Japan.

The Sunday prayer for simplicity read:

I will be simple as a child;
I'll labor to be meek and mild;
In this good work my time I'll spend,
And with my tongue I'll not offend. 🌿

If a man's mind becomes pure, his surroundings will also become pure.

— THE BUDDHA

God be thanked
that there are some
in the world to whose
hearts the barnacles
will not cling.

— Josiah Gilbert Holland

My dear child, if you desire
to be free from the cycle of birth
and death, then abandon the objects
of sense gratification as poison.
Drink instead the nectar of
forbearance, upright conduct,
mercy, cleanliness and truth.

— CHANAKYA

By two wings a man is
lifted up from things
earthly: by simplicity
and purity.

— THOMAS À KEMPIS

tranquility

When we are unable to find tranquility within ourselves, it is useless to seek it elsewhere.

— François de La Rochefoucauld

The Noh Actor

Gazing at the mirror before him, the Noh actor knocks silently on the doors of perception. Today he will make another attempt to leave behind the world of pretense and enter the elusive world of the Noh. The mask he holds in his hands is known as Ko-omote, the classical ideal of female beauty — serenely beyond human. He carved it himself. Expressionless as she now seems, on the stage together they will evoke the melancholy spirit of a sensitive poetess at the age of 15, drowning in the elegant futility of court life in 10th-century Japan.

Facing the mask, the man faces himself. The mask he carved now carves its way back into his soul. In the last silent moment before he walks onto the stage, he transcends thought and feeling, time and space. He becomes the mask, as the mask becomes the woman. Placing it on his face, he enters elusive territory, where mask and wearer merge. He glides on feet no longer entirely his own for "a glimpse of the eternal in a world of constant change."

See how nature — trees, flowers, grass —
grows in silence; see the stars, the moon
and the sun, how they move in silence.
We need silence to be able to touch souls.

— MOTHER TERESA

The poor long for riches,
the rich long for heaven,
but the wise long for
a state of tranquility.

— SWAMI RAMA

Poetry is the spontaneous overflow

of powerful feelings: it takes its origin

from emotion recollected in tranquility.

— WILLIAM WORDSWORTH

We live in a very tense society.
We are pulled apart … and we all need
to learn how to pull ourselves together ….
I think that at least part of the
answer lies in solitude.

— HELEN HAYES

It is only when we silence the blaring sounds of our daily existence that we can finally hear the whispers of truth that life reveals to us, as it stands knocking on the doorsteps of our hearts.

— K. T. Jong

A poet is a nightingale, who sits in darkness and sings to cheer its own solitude with sweet sounds.

— PERCY BYSSHE SHELLEY

There is the beauty of the moment
and of the moment gone.
I do not know which to prefer,
The beauty of inflections
Or the beauty of innuendos,
The blackbird whistling
Or just after.

— WALLACE STEVENS

Only in quiet waters do things

mirror themselves undistorted.

Only in a quiet mind

is adequate perception of the world.

— HANS MARGOLIUS

You owe it
to everyone you love
(including yourself)
to find pockets of
tranquility in your
busy world.

— GEORGES BERNANOS

It is neither wealth nor splendor; but tranquility and occupation, which give you happiness.

— THOMAS JEFFERSON

Language … has created

the word "loneliness" to express

the pain of being alone.

And it has created the word "solitude"

to express the glory of being alone.

— PAUL TILLICH

Snow in a Silver Bowl

At the time of the Renaissance in Europe,
a rebirth of the arts occurred in Japan half
a world away, in their Muromachi period.
Poetry and painting flourished, and a
unique and subtle form of theater called
Noh developed. This dramatic form used
exquisitely carved masks and combined
mime, dance, poetry, and song. Noh tells
stories of human passion and struggle
from an otherworldly perspective. With

enigmatic masks and subtle gestures, actors train for a lifetime to be able to communicate universal emotion to the audience.

The man who created this elegant art form was Zeami, who wrote the classic book of dramatic theory called the *Kaden-sho*. Through it he relates the secrets of achieving the heights of accomplishment as a Noh actor. With images from nature as a constant metaphor, Zeami refers to the various levels of artistic achievement in the performing arts as *hana*, or flowers.

One of the highest levels Zeami acknowledges is when an actor has captured a moment of beauty as crisp and austere as:

> *piling up snow in a silver bowl ... the hues that derive from a pure, clean white light, an appearance that gives rise to a real sense of gentleness — can it not be said that such represents the Flower of Tranquility?* 🌿

Humor is emotional
chaos remembered
in tranquility.

— JAMES THURBER

The mind is so rarely disturbed,

but that the company of a friend

will restore it to some degree

of tranquility and sedateness.

— ADAM SMITH

That which is false
troubles the heart,
but truth brings
joyous tranquility.

— RUMI

If you want inner peace find it in solitude, not speed, and if you would find yourself, look to the land from which you came and to which you go.

— STEWART L. UDALL

You must learn to be still in the midst of activity and to be vibrantly alive in repose.

— INDIRA GANDHI

Learn to be calm and
you will always be happy.

— Paramhansa Yogananda

Did you ever see an unhappy horse?

Did you ever see a bird that has the blues?

One reason why birds and horses are not

unhappy is because they are not trying

to impress other birds and horses.

— DALE CARNEGIE

It is an invincible greatness of mind
not to be elevated or dejected
with good or ill fortune.
A wise man is content with his lot,
whatever it be — without wishing
for what he has not.

— SENECA

No man should go through life
without once experiencing healthy,
even bored solitude in the wilderness,
finding himself depending solely on
himself and thereby learning his true
and hidden strength.

— JACK KEROUAC

One of the greatest
necessities in America
is to discover
creative solitude.

— CARL SANDBURG

I cannot walk through the suburbs
in the solitude of the night
without thinking that the night pleases us
because it suppresses idle details,
just as our memory does.

— JORGE LUIS BORGES

There are hundreds of tasks we feel we must accomplish in the day, but if we do not take them one at a time and let them pass through the day slowly and evenly, as do the grains of sand passing through the narrow neck of the hourglass, then we are bound to break our own physical and mental structure.

— DALE CARNEGIE

Never be afraid to sit
awhile and think.

— LORRAINE HANSBERRY

I feel within me a
peace above all earthly
dignities, a still and
quiet conscience.

— WILLIAM SHAKESPEARE

Like water, we are truest

to our nature in repose.

— CYRIL CONNOLLY

The fruit of silence
is tranquility.

— ARABIAN PROVERB

contentment

Many go fishing all their lives without knowing that it is not fish they are after.

— HENRY DAVID THOREAU

The Farmers' Festival

A thousand red-tailed dragonflies hang
suspended in midair over the rice fields,
making this humid summer day worthwhile.
Beyond the fields, a stand of golden bamboo
sways almost imperceptibly in what nearly
passes for a cooling breeze. The river beyond
it is invisible — there's only the sound of
rushing water. The mountain rises higher
than you can see from the long porch. In the
wooden shrine that haunts the enormous

tile-roofed farmhouse, family ghosts dwell silently.

It is the final night of the O-bon festival, and the spirits of ancestors have come once again for their annual visit from the other world. It has been good to have them here, those former keepers of this mountain village; good to place offerings, wash the headstones, and remember. Twilight brings a procession of farmers and their families up the road in their white utility trucks. At the temple on the hill, they join together for a night of camaraderie, sakè drinking, and singing the old songs together.

Stand outside the heavy wooden doors of the farmhouse, with a homesick foreigner's heart — not your village, not your country, not your ghosts. The voice of the village elder echoes down the valley walls with sounds as ancient as the hills. The old man sings for his father's father and for his children's children. But not for you.

Yet in the end it was enough to have witnessed this moment, to have heard those voices. You are content to know at last that the ancient spirits belong to no one and to all. 🌿

To the right, books;

to the left, a tea-cup.

In front of me, the fireplace;

behind me, the post.

There is no greater

happiness than this.

— Teiga

The secret of contentment is knowing how to enjoy what you have, and to be able to lose all desire for things beyond your reach.

— LIN YUTANG

Any so-called material thing that you want
is merely a symbol: you want it not for
itself, but because it will content your
spirit for the moment.

— MARK TWAIN

Money doesn't talk,

it swears.

— BOB DYLAN

What a miserable thing
life is: you're living in
clover, only the clover
isn't good enough.

— BERTOLT BRECHT

There is no greater curse than the lack of contentment; no greater sin than the desire for possession.

— LAO TSE

My crown is in my heart,

not on my head,

Nor decked with diamonds

and Indian stones,

Nor to be seen:

My crown is called content:

A crown it is, that seldom kings enjoy.

— WILLIAM SHAKESPEARE

If the book is good, is about something
that you know, and is truly written,
and reading it over you see that this is so,
you can let the boys yip and the noise will
have that pleasant sound coyotes make
on a very cold night when they are out
in the snow and you are in your own
cabin that you have built or paid for
with your work.

— ERNEST HEMINGWAY

Contentment is natural wealth; luxury is artificial poverty.

— SOCRATES

You can't have everything.

Where would you put it?

— STEVEN WRIGHT

To be content with little
is difficult; to be content
with much, impossible.

— MARIE E. ESCHENBACH

The Stone Water Basin

Ryoanji, one of Japan's most famous Zen temples, is renowned for its *karesansui* ("dry landscape" garden). Fifteen rocks of different shapes and sizes are positioned across a flat sea of raked gravel. From no single vantage point can all fifteen stones be seen. Many have attempted to decipher the ambiguous meaning of its composition. Is it a tiger fording a stream with her cubs, as popular legend suggests? Or is the garden simply another Zen vehicle for conveying the unknowable quality of the universe? It is spellbinding in its incomprehensibility. The designer died in 1525, and there is no one left to ask.

Behind the temple building adjacent to the garden sits an inconspicuous stone water basin, a *tsukubai*, used for rinsing the hands and mouth in a symbolic ritual of purification. The top of the basin is carved in the shape of a Chinese coin, with a square shape in the center. Aligned with the four sides of the square are four Chinese characters, which together form this ultimate Zen inscription:

> *Ware tada taru koto shiru.*
> [I only know contentment]. 🌿

Most men pursue

pleasure with such

breathless haste that

they hurry past it.

— Søren Kierkegaard

Besides the noble art of getting things done, there is the noble art of leaving things undone. The wisdom of life consists in the elimination of nonessentials.

— LIN YUTANG

The greatest wealth is to live content with little, for there is never want where the mind is satisfied.

— LUCRETIUS

I don't want to own anything
that won't fit into my coffin.

— FRED ALLEN

What makes us discontented with our condition is the absurdly exaggerated idea we have of the happiness of others.

— FRENCH PROVERB

To feel that one has
a place in life solves
half the problems of
contentment.

— GEORGE E. WOODBERRY

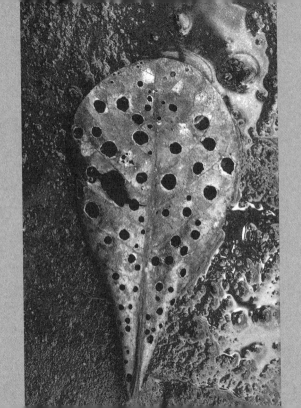

When you can think of yesterday without regret and tomorrow without fear, you are near contentment.

— UNKNOWN

Be happy with what
you have and are, be
generous with both,
and you won't have to
hunt for happiness.

— WILLIAM E. GLADSTONE

If thou wouldst be happy
… have an indifference
for more than what
is sufficient.

— WILLIAM PENN

You buy furniture. You tell yourself,
this is the last sofa I will ever need
in my life. Buy the sofa, then for a couple
years you're satisfied that no matter what
goes wrong, at least you've got your sofa
issue handled. Then the right set of dishes.
Then the perfect bed. The drapes. The rug.
Then you're trapped in your lovely nest,
and the things you used to own,
now they own you.

— CHUCK PALAHNIUK

He is rich who is
content with the least;
for contentment is the
wealth of nature.

— SOCRATES

Economy, prudence, and a simple life

are the sure masters of need, and will often

accomplish that which their opposites,

with a fortune at hand, will fail to do.

— CLARA BARTON

Give me neither poverty nor riches, but give me contentment.

— HELEN KELLER

Yes, there is a Nirvanah; it is leading your sheep to a green pasture, and in putting your child to sleep, and in writing the last line of your poem.

— KAHLIL GIBRAN

Acknowledgments

My deepest thanks, first of all, go to the amazing people I knew in Kyoto. They taught me, through the example of their lives, about wabi and sabi, and about the many different ways there are to live life and enjoy it. Some of those whose stories appear in this book are gone now, and some preferred to be anonymous. Here's to you then, the many who have shared your knowledge: the tea teachers, the artists, the craftsmen, the housewives, the historians, and the Buddhist priests. Your lessons have not been lost or forgotten. Please know how much I appreciate your many kindnesses.

I am extremely grateful to John Einarsen, photographer and founding editor of *Kyoto Journal*. John not only contributed many moving photographs that grace the pages of this book, he also offered encouragement at a time when I knew this book was just going to be too much.

Sincere thanks to Robert Singer for more than 20 years of friendship and encouragement. Curator of Japanese Art at the Los Angeles County Museum of Art, Robert shared a quiet Kyoto neighborhood with me for many years. Special thanks also to his wife, Jennifer Boynton, who contributed valuable suggestions to the final manuscript.

My thanks go to Deborah Balmuth and Pam Art at

Storey Publishing for bringing the idea for this book to me, and convincing me that I could do it. It took me down a path I needed to walk and helped bring my experience in Japan to full circle. Thanks to Nancy Wood for her patience and enthusiasm in editing this book through its many incarnations. Thank you to Kent Lew and Karen Beck for the special efforts required to design and illustrate a book on this subject. Thank you very much to Eri Takase for the artistry of her elegant calligraphy.

My love and thanks go also to my late father, Bill Durston, who tried to remind me more than once to slow down and live. He was a talented artist and photographer who never failed to see the beauty in each passing day.

Last, but most of all, here's to you, Stephen Futscher, my husband and partner, for the many days of research you gave to the quotations that make this book special — time lost to the creation of your own art. Thank you, too, for the photographs you contributed, particularly for the picture of the little alleyway in Horiike-cho, where we both lived so long and happily. Thank you always for your support and love. 🍃

Related Reading

Aitken, Robert. A Zen Harvest. New York: Weatherhill, 1992.

Holmes, Stewart W. Zen Art for Meditation. Tokyo: Tuttle, 1978.

Itoh, Teiji. The Essence of Japanese Beauty. Tokyo: Mazda Motor
    Corp., 1993.

Keene, Donald. Essays in Idleness: The Tsurezuregusa of Kenko.
    Tokyo: Tuttle, 1989.

Koren, Leonard. Wabi-Sabi for Artists, Designers, Poets & Philoso-
    phers. Berkeley: Stonebridge Press, 1994.

Munsterberg, Hugo. Zen & Oriental Art. Tokyo: Tuttle, 1993.

Okakura, Kakuzo. The Book of Tea. Tokyo: Tuttle, 1972.

Okakura, Kakuzo. The Ideals of the East. New York: ICG Muse,
    2002.

Plutschow, Herbert E. Historical Chanoyu. Tokyo: The Japan
    Times, 1986.

Sen, Soshitsu XV. *Tea Life, Tea Mind*. Tokyo: Weatherhill, 1987.

Sprigg, June. *By Shaker Hands*. New York: Alfred A. Knopf, 1979.

Suzuki, Daisetsu T. *Zen and Japanese Culture*. Bollingen, 1959.

Tanizaki, Junichiro. *In Praise of Shadows*. Tokyo: Tuttle, 1984.

Thoreau, Henry David. *Walden*. 1854.

Ueda, Makoto. *Zeami, Basho, Yeats, Pound*. Paris: Mouton & Co., 1965.

Warner, Langdon. *The Enduring Art of Japan*. New York: Grove Press, 1988.

Watts, Alan W. *The Spirit of Zen*. New York: Grove Weidenfeld, 1960.

Winokur, Jon. *Zen to Go*. New York: Plume, 1990.

Photography Credits

Source Credits

For permission to use copyrighted or protected material,
we thank the following literary executors and publishers.
We have made every effort to obtain permission to reprint
material in this book and to publish proper acknowledgments. We regret any error or oversight.

6, 23: *Zen and Senryu* by Alan Watts. © 2004 by Alan Watts,
published by Locust Publishing.

8, 24: *Zeami, Basho, Yeats, Pound: A Study in Japanese and
English Poetics* by Makoto Ueda. © 1965 by Makoto Ueda,
published by Mouton.

17: *In Praise of Shadows* by Tanizaki Junichiro. © 1980 by
Tanizaki Junichiro, published by Leetes Island Books.

22, 72: *Essays in Idleness: The Tsurezuregusa of Kenko*, trans. by

Donald Keene. © 1998 by Donald Keene, published by Columbia University Press.

29: *Melancholy Objects: On Photography* by Susan Sontag. © 2001 by Susan Sontag, published by Picador Publishing.

49: "Heroic Reason," *Selected Writings of Juan Ramon Jimenez*, trans. by H. R. Hays. © 1999 by H. R. Hays, published by Farrar, Straus, and Giroux.

51: *Little Essays* by George Santayana. © 1920 by George Santayana, published by Constable Publishing.

52: "A Total Eclipse of Reason" by John Rennie. *Scientific American*, November 1999. © 1999 by John Rennie, published by *Scientific American*.

61: *The Open Door* by Helen Keller. © 1957 by Helen Keller, published by Double Day Publishing.

76, 159: *The Summing Up* by William Somerset Maugham.

116: *Sadhana: The Realization of Life* by Rabindranath Tagore. © 1942 by Rabindranath Tagore, published by Kessinger Publishing.

122: *Zorba the Greek* by Nikos Kazantzakis. © 1996 by Nikos Kazantzakis, published by Touchstone/1st Scribner Paperback Fiction.

139: *Miss Manners' Guide to Excruciatingly Correct Behavior* by Judith Martin. © 1979 by Judith Martin, published by W. W. Norton and Company.

149: *Albert Einstein, the Human Side: New Glimpses from His Archives*, ed. by Helen Dukas and Banesh Hoffman. © 1989, published by Princeton University Press.

151: *The Selfish Gene* by Richard Dawkins. © 1990 by Richard Dawkins, published by Oxford University Press.

161: *Principles of Social Reconstruction* by Bertrand Russell.

297: *The Theory of Moral Sentiments* by Adam Smith. © 2002 by Adam Smith, published by Cambridge University Press.

299: *The Quiet Crisis* by Stewart L. Udall. © 1991 by Stewart L. Udell, published by Gibbs Smith Publishing.

304: *Lonesome Traveler* by Jack Kerouac. © 1985 by Jack Kerouac, published by Grove Press.

307: *Labyrinths: Selected Stories and Other Writings* by Jorge Luis Borges. © 1964 by Jorge Luis Borges, published by New Directions Publishing.

308: *How to Stop Worrying and Start Living* by Dale Carnegie. © 1990 by Dale Carnegie, published by Pocket Publishing.

309: *A Raisin in the Sun* by Lorraine Hansberry. © 1995 by Lorraine Hansberry, published by Modern Library Publishing.

331: *Enemies of Promise* by Cyril Connolly. © 1996 by Cyril Connelly, published by Persea Books.

326: "It's Alright, Ma (I'm Only Bleeding)," *Bringing it All Back Home* by Bob Dylan. © 1994 by Bob Dylan, published by SONY.

327: *Jungle of Cities and Other Plays* by Bertolt Brecht. © 1996 by Bertolt Brecht, published by Grove Press.

330: *Hemingway* by Carlos Baker. © 1972 by Carlos Baker, published by Princeton University Press.

348: *Fight Club* by Chuck Palahniuk. © 1996 by Chuck Palahniuk, published by W. W. Norton and Company.

DIANE DURSTON is the author of *Old Kyoto* and *Kyoto: Seven Paths to the Heart of the City,* two books the *New York Times* has called "classics!" She lived in Kyoto for 18 years, where she served as cultural consultant on Japan for corporations, universities, and museums, including the National Gallery of Art in Washington, D.C.